Before You Speak

UNDERSTANDING THE POWER OF WORDS

Jessica McNeil

WESTBOW
PRESS®
A DIVISION OF THOMAS NELSON
& ZONDERVAN

WestBow Press books may be ordered through booksellers or by contacting:

WestBow Press
A Division of Thomas Nelson & Zondervan
1663 Liberty Drive
Bloomington, IN 47403
www.westbowpress.com
1 (866) 928-1240

Cover photos by: Christopher Mitchell Photography

ISBN: 978-1-9736-9064-1 (sc)
ISBN: 978-1-9736-9063-4 (e)

Print information available on the last page.

WestBow Press rev. date: 7/20/2020

I dedicate this first book to my mother, Zena Melissa Graham. She gave me Jesus, and the rest is history. Through all my life she taught me that wisdom is the principal thing, and in all my getting get an understanding. My mom also taught me effective communication, even though it took me a long time to use it. Still working on it every day. I had no idea that my journaling (compliments of my mom) would bring about becoming an author. Thank you, mommy, for always praying for me and only expecting my best. Thank you to my husband, Jeffrey and my beautiful daughters, Judah, Jewel, and Joy for going on this writing journey with me. I appreciate the time to pray, research, and study. The best is yet to come!

Love you to life,

Jessica

Table of Contents

Preface

We have all heard the saying "sticks and stones may break my bones, but words will never hurt me." I'm sure those who have been negatively affected by comments and conversations would disagree. By the same token, words can bring affirmation and empowerment. Whichever way we decide to use our words, they hold great weight.

In Psalm 141:3 NIV, David asked God to put a guard on his mouth and set a watch at the door at his lips. When we acknowledge God in our speech, He will give us direction.

"A man's belly is satisfied by the fruit of his mouth; and with the increase of his lips shall he be filled. Death and life are in the power of the tongue: those who love it shall eat the fruit thereof."

Proverbs 18:20-21 KJV

The very words we speak can be poison or nourishment. Nourishment revitalizes and causes life to continue to grow. Poison contaminates, bringing on pain and possibly death.

We have to decide what we want our words to accomplish; edification or destruction.

Words clearly have power. We must own the effects and consequences of the words we release. Every word spoken will have to be accounted for. This book is going to help bring light on how powerful words are and how to make better use of the words we speak. As you go through this book, reflect on the times that words negatively or positively changed your life. Make a decision to change your speech accordingly. Remember change is a process. Allow the words hereafter to help guide you in the process of considering and understanding the power of your words before you speak.

Introduction

"But I say unto you every idle word that man shall speak; they shall give account thereof in the day of judgment. For by thy words thou shalt be justified, and by thy words thou shalt be condemned."

Matthew 12: 36-37 KJV

The passage gives some simple yet powerful advice. These words were Jesus' way of bringing clarity and admonishment to the Pharisees. Jesus had just performed the miracle of casting out a demon and healing a man. After being falsely accused by religious leaders, Jesus took time to address the situation. In this case the Pharisees allowed their inner issues to be released through words.

"...for of the abundance of the heart the mouth speaks."

Luke 6:45 KJV

Like the Pharisees, we too have a tendency of releasing out of our mouths what is in our heart. Oftentimes in an instant, our inner thoughts and emotions spill out revealing our true perspective, our true heart.

"Keep thy heart with all diligence; for out of it are the issues of life."

Proverbs 4:23 KJV

"But those things which proceed out of the mouth come forth from the heart; and they defile the man."

Matthew 15:18 KJV

They were upset by the works that Jesus was able to perform and accused him of receiving his power from Satan. We know that when things out of the ordinary occur, some people gravitate toward the thing, while others reject it. Questions tend to arise to disprove the situation. They were unable to explain or comprehend and as a result they became frustrated and jealous.

The outcome of every comment is directly related to the source from which it was released. The person who released the remarks is always held accountable. That is why it is imperative that we watch what leaves our mouths.

"But I say unto you every idle word that man shall speak; they shall give account thereof in the day of judgment. For by thy words thy shalt be justified, and by thy words thou shalt be condemned."

Matthew 12: 36-37 KJV

I know the concept seems simple, but it's easier said than done. I have dealt with the effects of unguarded words on both ends. Once I began to change my speech, I noticed there was a change. I became aware of the significance of my words. It was not until I gained an understanding of why there was a change and how I could control certain situations in my life that the true change came.

We must learn to train our tongues to speak The Word which will benefit our lives on every level. God honors His word above all His name. When we take Him at His Word and speak The Word, we will see improvements.

Everybody wants their life to become better or move forward. The way we choose to talk can make a major difference. We have to take accountability for what we say.

I encourage taking time to study The Word, pray and speak God's Word over your life. It's time to gain knowledge and understanding of how to change our world with our words, before we speak.

Definition

"Wisdom is the principal thing; therefore, get wisdom: and with all thy getting get understanding."

Proverbs 4:7 KJV

When my two oldest were toddlers they made this verse clear, in a comical sense. Judah, the oldest was so distraught about something Jewel had done. Judah called me over and over to say that Jewel was being nosey. Mind you they are about 2 and 3. I am thinking "how do you know what nosey means?" I wanted an understanding of what she meant by nosey. I asked her "What is Jewel doing?" Judah said loud and proud "she is digging in her nose!" I laughed and then I had to think about how easy it is to misinterpret what someone is saying.

We must be careful of what we say and how we say it. Always get an understanding. When you have an understanding, the information can be used in the most effective way. These days information is right at the tip of our fingers, literally.

It is great to gain knowledge and have a plethora of information in your arsenal. What good will all of the information do if it is not understood?

Not only that, how can the material be effectively used without clarity? The information is supplied for application. That is like having bullets but never putting them into the gun. It's useless. It is not enough for us to ascertain the direction God's Word gives; we have to actually follow the directions.

You have magnified Your word above all Your name. Psalm 138:2 NKJV. You will find scriptures at the end that reference the content that is discussed throughout this book. Use them during your prayer and meditation. When we give God His Word, He will honor it. God's Word goes forth to accomplish what it is set to do. Effectively praying and applying God's Word brings results. Give God His Word and watch it come to pass. He is faithful, but we must use His Word for Him to honor it.

In order to grasp this information, there must be understanding. Below is a list of terms that will be frequently used. They have been placed at the beginning to establish a foundation as well as for ease of access.

The black bulleted words are the main vocabulary being used; the white bulleted words are an expansion on the meaning of the main vocabulary. The terms and definitions are going to be used throughout the book.

- <u>decree</u>- an official order or decision
  - o <u>official</u>- position of authority; authoritative
  - o <u>authority</u>-the power or right to command, act

- <u>establish</u>- to order, enact permanently; to set up; to cause to be; bring about; to demonstrate, to prove
  - o <u>be</u>- to exist; live; to happen; to occur

- <u>light</u> n.- illumination; a thing used to ignite something; knowledge; enlightenment; aspect adj.- to come into existence; to come to public view; to understand
- <u>atmosphere</u>-the air surrounding the earth; a pervading mood or spirit; general effect
  - o <u>pervading</u>- to spread throughout or be prevalent throughout
  - o <u>prevalent</u>-generally used; widely existing
  - o <u>effect</u>- brought about by cause; result; influence; an impression made on the mind; accomplish

- <u>climate</u>- the prevailing weather condition of a place
  - o <u>prevailing</u>- superior in influence

- <u>pattern</u>- a regular way of acting or doing; a predictable way of thinking
- <u>process</u>- continual development involving many changes.

Word Power

"Thou shall <u>decree a thing</u>, and it shall <u>be established</u> unto thee, and the <u>light</u> shall shine upon thy <u>ways</u>."

Job 22:28 KJV

We are discussing the results of our speech, so this is a verbal decree. We have the power to decide what to speak about a person, incident, or concern. Everything that is spoken will occur and it will be known to all, what we permit to lead our thoughts. Whether our thoughts are pure and positive, or perverse and negative, it will be clear which has control.

Our words are able to set situations and circumstances in motion. Genesis Chapter 1 gives several examples of how God did just that.

"And God <u>said</u>, let there be light: and there was light. And God saw the light, that <u>it was good;</u>"

Genesis 1:3-4 KJV

"And God <u>said</u>, let there be a firmament in the midst of the waters, and let and let it divide the waters from the waters. And God made the firmament and divided the waters which were under the firmament from the waters which were above the firmament: and <u>it was so</u>."

Gen 1:6-7 KJV

"And God <u>said</u>, Let the waters under the heaven be gathered together unto one place, and let the dry land appear: and <u>it was so</u>."

Gen 1:9 KJV

As we continue to read the text the same two phrases are repeated "God *said*" and "*it was so.*" God spoke and His words were created. The very thing that God spoke became visible and tangible in the atmosphere.

Even Jesus exercised this authority during his time upon the Earth. As he performed great miracles, His words alone created results. Jesus walked in the magnitude of power that His father gave him and it became clear to a centurion man how powerful words are.

"The centurion answered and said, Lord, I am not worthy that thou shouldest come under my roof: but speak the word only, and my servant shall be healed."

Matthew 8:8 KJV

Ezekiel was another that spoke with authority. He was given words to speak directly from the mouth of God. The words brought life to a dead situation. Literally!

"The hand of the Lord was upon me, and carried me out in the spirit of the Lord, and set me down in the midst of the valley which was full of bones,² And caused me to pass by them roundabout: and, behold, there were very many in the open valley; and, lo, they were very dry.³ And he said unto me, Son of man, can these bones live? And I answered, O Lord God, thou knowest.⁴ Again he said unto me, Prophesy upon these bones, and say unto these bones, and say unto them, O ye dry bones, hear the word of the Lord.⁵ Thus saith the Lord God unto these bones; Behold, I will cause breath to enter into you, and ye shall live:⁶ And I will lay sinew upon you, and will bring flesh upon you, and cover you with skin, and put breath in you, and ye shall live; and ye shall know that I am the Lord. ⁷

So, I prophesied as I was commanded: and as I prophesied, there was a noise, and behold a shaking, and the bones came together, bone to his bone. ⁸*And when I beheld, lo, the sinews and the flesh came up upon them, and then skin covered them above: but there was no breath in them.* ⁹ *Then said he unto me, Prophesy unto the wind, prophesy, son of man, and say to the wind, thus saith the Lord God; Come from the four winds, O breath, and breathe upon these slain, that they may live.* ¹⁰

So, I prophesied as he commanded me, and the breath came into them, and they lived, and stood up upon their feet, an exceeding great army. ¹¹ *Then he said unto me, Son of Man, these bones are the whole house of Israel: behold, they say, our bones are dried, and our hope is lost: we are cut off for our parts.* ¹² *Therefore prophesy and say unto them, Thus saith the Lord God; Behold, O my people, I will open your graves, and cause you to come up out of your graves, and bring you into the land of Israel.* ¹³ *And ye shall know that I am the Lord, when I have opened your graves, O my people, and brought you up out of your graves,* ¹⁴ *And shall put my spirit in you, and ye shall live, and I shall place you in your own land: then shall ye know that I the Lord have spoken it, and performed it, saith the Lord."*

Ezekiel 37: 1-14 KJV

What great displays of faith and demonstration of God's power. Guess what? God has allotted us the same power and authority. He has given us His Word and it works as we apply it.

God provides us with multiple ways to receive His Word; the bible, revelation by His Spirit, and even hearing His voice. The Word of God is powerful and sharp.

We have to take advantage of the tools we are given. Access the power and begin to speak with power and authority concerning your life.

Make this declaration over your life by faith. Read the following proclamation aloud to affirm the change that you are about to visibly witness.

God, I surrender my mind, my will, and my emotions to you. Search me, O' God, and know my heart: try me and know my thoughts. Through you, Jesus, I have a clean heart and a right spirit renewed within me. God I am letting my old thoughts and words pass away, make them new. God you have given me the tongue of the learned. I am endowed with new speech patterns.

God, I renounce the carnal mindset, which is death, and I take on the mind of the spirit, which is life and peace. The mind that is in Christ is also in me, Lord.

God thank you for allowing me to learn a more excellent way to speak; and how to use the power that You have given me to take dominion over the airways of my life.

I renounce every negative word that bred stagnation, apathy, fear, death, and destruction over my life. I denounce any words that created a world of depression. My life has been changed. I overcome by the Blood of the Lamb and by the word of my testimony.

I will not accept anything contrary to Your plans for my life to be spoken over me. Every tongue that rises against me, falsely in judgment, I shall condemn. I hold every thought and vain imagination captive, and I render them null and void. I surrender my cogitations to You Lord. I yield to You God. You are my Wonderful Counselor. Teach me to speak the way of the righteous.

My words will flow forth in a more excellent way because You have given me the tongue of the learned. My heart is applied to instruction and my ears to words of knowledge.

My mouth will speak wisdom as my heart meditates on understanding.

I will use discretion when I speak and my lips will keep knowledge. I am transformed by the renewing of my mind.

My speech will prove the good, acceptable, and perfect will of You, God.

Increase my faith as I meditate on your word day and night. I will study to answer as the righteous, that I may speak a word in season. I call those things that be not as though they were. I will speak and it will be done because I have the power to decree a thing and it will be established.

Greater is He that is in me than he that is in the world. Father, let the words of my mouth and the meditation of my heart be acceptable in thy sight. O Lord my strength and my redeemer. I make this declaration in **Jesus'** name, Amen.

Shift

The words spoken into our lives become the superior influence on our mind. As the same things are spoken over and over again we begin to rehearse them in our minds. In no time, we have memorized the statements and they become part of our regular thoughts and speech.

The days of allowing ourselves to accept everything that is spoken into our lives is over. It is time to create a verbal shift. We have to exercise authority over our atmosphere. Speaking the Word of God into our lives and receiving impartations of the Holy Spirit helps us to regain control by standing strong in the Lord and in the power of His might.

We have to learn to train our speech. In James 3:4-5 KJV, the Word of God explains how a great ship tossed by fierce wind is controlled by a small helm; similar to our tongue. Our tongue is but a small member of our body, yet it is so powerful. If you read a little further, the scripture says the tongue defiles the whole body. The Word of God is our hope.

Proverbs 4:20-22 KJV tells us that the word of God is life to those who find it and health to their flesh. The key to shifting is to **find** God's word pertaining to your situation and employ it. We have to actively search and dig for what we need in God's word before the shift can begin. God's word never fails and we can trust that His word will accomplish what we send it to do. Take God at His word.

We have to declare Psalms 39:1 ERV and say "I will be careful about what I say. I will not let my tongue cause me to sin." We profess, "I am purposed that my mouth shall not transgress," like David in Psalms 17:3 KJV.

Ephesians 4:29 GNB says plain and clear; "Do not use harmful words, but only helpful words, the kind that build up and provide what is needed, so that what you say will do good to those who hear you."

Gaining an understanding of God's Word and His will for our lives, allows us to obtain the power to make the transition. It is time to make a change.

The process starts with a decision. We have to surrender everything to Christ and allow Him to lead as we learn to perfect our speech. Let us decree the decision into the atmosphere.

"Thou shall decree a thing, and it shall be established unto thee, and the light shall shine upon thy ways."

Job 22:28 KJV

We have to decide what type of atmosphere we want to have; what type of verbal climate we want to live in. The manner in which we choose to spread our words will influence our days.

If we continue to speak in such a way, those words can become a superior influence in our lives.

"For he spake, and it was done…"

Psalm 33:9 KJV

I have dealt with the reality of this on a personal level. We overcome by the blood of the lamb and the word of our testimony. I had to come to grips with reality. My words created and shifted my atmosphere.

About 10 years ago I faced a situation that made this all relevant. There was a particular person that I was around frequently that would often have random spurts of wrath filled with negative language. One of the things that I complained about was their short temper that was usually accompanied with harsh language.

A barrage of cruel words would come out. Sometimes I did not know why. It seemed to me that it was just to be mean. If I was singing or dancing to music, they would turn it off. When I decided to read my bible and the person felt I should or could be doing something else, they would knock it from my hand or take it.

I would sit and cry about it silently as I went on to do other things. The individual would walk by and tell me "nobody cares if you are crying," and walk away. It was extreme! This occurred over a series of years.

I was hurt and confused after each encounter that involved the negativity. I shut down and questioned my life, my faith, and God. The words they spoke were death- killing my joy, my peace, my confidence, and literally shook my faith.

In my mind, they reminded me of the Grinch. Every time they would lose their cool, I would call them the "Grinch." I would go as far as to even sing the song. Now mind you, I would not say it directly to them; I would wait until we were no longer around one another. Either way, the words were still spoken and released into the atmosphere.

After a period of time I started noticing that the situation became worse; the surges of anger became more frequent. The more I spoke about how they "always" did this and they "never" did that; it became my reality. I used my authority to create and allow discord to continue to ruin my joy and my relationship with them.

Just take a moment to think about some of the things that have been spoken concerning you; whether or not you were the one speaking. More often than not, were the words manifested? I had to learn to change my language and how I respond to situations. I am continually perfecting that skill; it did not happen quickly, and I did not change overnight. During this process I questioned God. I wanted to know why. Why me? What did I do?

After I sobbed for a while God asked me if I was done. He proceeded to tell me that it was not for me. God taught me to speak life by decreeing and declaring His words. He taught me how to be strong in prayer by taking to heart His word and trusting that He would not disappoint me.

Understand, we have been given the power to decree and establish our future. We do not have to accept the negative words that we or others speak over our lives.

The movement for change began when we were being taught about "the atmosphere" at church. I had to stop and retrace my words; that is when I was able to see what my words had created.

Some of the things that I encountered were intensified by my untrained language. The more I used derogatory words to describe the individual they began to further embody what I said.

I saw my words about this person began to manifest before me. As I spoke, my words created a reality that I was not pleased with. I started to realize how powerful words were. Every time I said "always" about the individual's behavior I was reaffirming that things were going to stay the same. When I said "never" about what they were not doing at the time, I shut down the opportunity for them to start doing something different or new.

I came to the understanding that I had to transform my speech in order for my atmosphere to change. I wanted that person to be joyful, loving, and speaking pleasant things, so I had to adjust my words to alter my circumstance. In order to change the way we speak, the way we think has to change.

There is an option; we have to make a decision. Glory be to God I have not and will not speak of the "Grinch" anymore. I allowed God to teach me to shift my speech.

The things that we focus our minds on tend to shape our vocabulary. We have got to make up our mind to change our mindset. A mindset is the way in which thinking, reasoning, and intellect are established; our regular thought pattern.

"For to be carnally minded is death; but to be spiritually minded is life and peace."

Romans 8:6 KJV

We must begin to have a more excellent way of thinking. We cannot allow ourselves to be stuck in a pattern of thinking that is not conducive to God's will for our lives. We should just do away with patterned thinking.

A pattern repeats and is consecutive. A B A B; after one repetition it's clear that after A comes...B.

Elementary, right? Many times, we allow our thoughts to do the same thing. They become so predictable.

When we get blessed, we are happy, or when a trial comes, we get upset or discouraged. It is good to be blessed, but we have far greater and longer lasting blessings when we endure the hardships.

"We have small troubles for a while now, but these troubles are helping us gain an eternal glory. That eternal glory is much greater than our troubles," according to 2 Corinthians 4:17 ERV

"For our light affliction, which is but for a moment, worketh for us a far more exceeding and eternal weight of glory."

2 Corinthians 4:17 KJV

In order to get to the greater things and really experience the glory of God we have to break the pattern. Going back to patterns, there are more letters in the alphabet after a and b. Push past where you are! Take the limitations off!

We all have to do something different if we expect our results to be different. We are supposed to go from glory to glory, and from faith to faith. As we elevate our minds and thoughts our words will align. Once we change our words our lives will begin to change.

Colossians 3:2 NKJV reminds us to set our minds on things above and not on the things of the earth. At times we do not even notice when the change happens. The change happens as different things are introduced into our lives. Our thoughts gradually alter as we pick up words and phrases here and there. Before we know it, we have reconstructed our thoughts and speech.

Our speech can change for the better. Take an hourglass for instance: At first glance you barely notice that the grains are flowing down. After some time, a hill of sand becomes visible in the lower half of the glass. We have to start somewhere. The best way to do that is to go to the source: our thoughts.

Our thoughts take place in our mind. Once we continue in a certain way, we form a pattern. Our minds get set to an accustomed way of thinking. We have to be careful with our mindset.

Mindset

Where do we draw from to get the statements that we speak? That is easy, our thoughts. As our thoughts accumulate, we form a mindset. It is your way of thinking or frame of mind.

Changing our mindset is how we achieve improved results in our speech. When we change the way we think, we can change the way we speak, and it is then that we will see things change in our lives. The way we begin to do that is to change our way of thinking and talking in everyday situations. Once we learn to do that, when difficult times arise, we are prepared and know what approach to take. We have to get rid of the old way of thinking. Let us fully make the change and embrace a new way of thinking.

Luke gives a great illustration of how the old and new do not work well together. Luke 5:37 MSG says "No one cuts up a fine silk scarf to patch old work clothes; you want the fabrics to match. And you don't put wine in old, cracked bottles; you get strong, clean bottles for your fresh vintage wine. And no one who has ever tasted fine aged wine prefers unaged wine."

Jesus explains to a group of staunch, pretentious religious leaders called Pharisees, that old and new do not go well together. It is impossible to remain in one state of mind and change it at the same time. When we look at James 3:10 CEV, it says "my dear friends, with our tongues we speak both praises and curses. We praise our Lord and Father, and we curse people who were created to be like God, and this is not right."

"A double minded man is unstable in all his ways."

James 1:8 KJV

We cannot just decree God's Word and our desires into the atmosphere without a different or renewed mindset. We must trust in God's Word and have faith, believing that it will come to pass. God's Word says the promise is received by faith. His Word is the promise that we must have faith in. We have to rid ourselves of any and all thoughts contrary to that.

"Casting down imaginations, and every high thing that exalteth itself against the knowledge of God and bringing into captivity every thought to the obedience of Christ;"

2 Corinthians 10:5 KJV

It is time out for negative thinking. There are many things that we face and temptations that come our way, but we have a choice. If we do not capture these thoughts we will give them authority in our lives. Only God's Word is supposed to reign supreme, if we allow. We have a will.

We have to be determined to believe the report of the Lord no matter what anyone has to say. We are the head and not the tail, above only and not beneath, the lender and not the borrower. We can do all things through Christ who strengthens us.

Greater is He that is within us than he that is in the world. We have to boldly speak His Word. Our thoughts have to be focused on better things.

"Finally, brethren, whatsoever things are true, whatsoever things are honest, whatsoever things are just, whatsoever things are pure, whatsoever things are lovely, whatsoever things are of good report; if there be any virtue, and if there be any praise, think on these things."

Philippians 4:8 KJV

Paul makes it so simple; we have to program our minds with better things. The things that we think on tend to determine what we say. Impure, false, lying, hateful, and negative reports cannot yield progressive thinking. There has to be some good seeds planted into our minds in order for the fruits of good speech to grow.

It is not enough to just hear one good thought or speak one positive word; we have to make them a constant meditation. God's Word is filled with great promises and blessings that He has for us.

We are to meditate on God's Word day and night according to Joshua 1:8 NIV. As we rehearse it, it becomes a part of us and we exude the Word of God in every area. The more we allow His Word to shape our thoughts we cannot help but speak like God as well.

Sometimes circumstances may seem to be ill-timed or even bad. Things are not always what they seem, and they do not have to be. We have the power to change these situations with our words.

I can remember a time when we lived in a 2-bedroom apartment. We had been playing catch up from my husband being laid off. I was a stay at home mom with 3 young children and little to no transportation. The space was overcrowded to say the least. As you could imagine the walls started closing in on me. If that were not enough, we received an eviction notice.

The previous managers knew our situation and were working with us to pay off the debt. Our complex came under new management. We had to pay what we owed within 60 days and move. These new people did not know us or care about our situation or previous arrangement. Now the new dilemma was figuring out what to do. If we paid the money, we would not have anything left to move.

My husband was in a new job, so we didn't have a lot of income. On top of that I was not working. If I did work, I would have to pay for daycare for 3 children under the age of 5. I whined and complained for a day or so. My negative words made me more discouraged.

One day I just cried out to God in frustration. I was searching for answers and a strategy. It was when I started speaking of God's words that I saw results. I declared, "God you said, you would never leave me nor forsake me." "God you said you would withhold no good thing from those that walk upright before you." "God you said you would give me the desires of my heart if I delight in you." "God you cannot lie, do what you said." "Show me Lord that you are for me." The more I spoke the better I felt. I chose to speak positive words of God's promises instead of rehearsing what was wrong. When I changed my speech, God brought a change to our situation.

Someone approached my husband about his excellent works at the hospital and asked him to work for them. My husband now had a job at the hospital and working for a man cleaning and painting houses.

This man owned more than 40 properties and offered my husband a chance to work on them when he had time. Hallelujah! That was just the start.

One day while I was tending to the children, just playing some games, Judah said "God's gonna give us a house." Judah was 4 years old at the time. I was baffled for a moment. I was like, what did you say? She repeated the exact sentence the same way. Honestly, at that time I was like ok, Lord is that you? Oh, was it ever!

Unbeknownst to me, my husband had been talking to the gentleman with the property about us needing to move. He shared with him that I wanted to move into an area with better schools because our children were coming to that age. So, when I told him about what Judah said, he was ready to talk.

The man had told my husband he had a property in the area where I wanted to move, if we wanted to see it. Without hesitation, I said yes!

We packed up the kids and went to see the house. It was nice on the outside, big backyard. The house had 3 bedrooms, 2 bathrooms, a huge living room, eat in kitchen, dining room and laundry room. God had exceeded our expectations. We moved in with no down payment. The icing on the cake was my husband and the gentleman had become partners in managing the properties. We were able to make payments each month when we had it. Not only that, but when we didn't have the payment, we were able to exchange work on another property for our payment.

God reminded me once again, we have the power to change our lives with our words. It requires faith and believing with your words. Even our prayers and petitions to God are words. When we speak God's word, we speak His existence into our situation. He is His word! We have to understand things are not always what they seem. When we trust that God will do what He said He will do, and speak it, it will come to pass.

God's promise to Abraham is another great testament of a spoken promise manifested by faith. There is a promise for each of us and we can receive it when we speak by faith to claim it.

"As it is written, I have made thee a father of many nations, before him whom he believed, even God, who quickeneth the dead, and calleth those things that be not as though they were. Who against hope believed in hope, that he might become the father of many nations; according to that which was spoken, So shall thy seed be. And being not weak in faith, he considered not his own body now dead, when he was about an hundred years old, neither yet the

deadness of Sara's womb: He staggered not at the promise of God through unbelief; but was strong in faith, giving glory to God; And being fully persuaded that, what he had promised, he was able also to perform."

Romans 4: 17- 21 KJV

Paul used Abraham as an example in this text. God told Abram that he would be the father of many nations. As we continue to read on in Genesis 17:5 NIV, we hear of the great things to come. Abraham receives a name change and multiple blessings, but he had faith that God would fulfill His word.

At that time, he was not the father of many nations. In fact, his wife was barren, so there was no possible way for the two of them to have a child without God.

Abraham trusted God. He didn't keep talking about what he could not do or what he did not have. He put his trust in the Lord. We cannot afford to suffer from doubt and unbelief. Abraham, instead of doubting, increased his faith. He took God at His word.

God spoke into existence with Abraham and Sara, what had not yet occurred. God decreed posterity over Abraham and life to Sara's womb. God is able to perform everything that He promises. God always honors His Word. Sara and Abraham were way past child bearing years, but the promise came to pass. They conceived the promised son and named him Isaac.

He has given us the power to do the same. We may not be 100 % in health, but we can decree that by the stripes of Jesus we are healed and divine wholeness is our portion. Our pocket may be running low; but God meets all our needs according to His riches in glory which is in Christ Jesus.

Speak the things that be not as though they currently are. We have to speak better results into existence by the power of God within us.

Things may not be where they should be, but we must speak the truth of God's word regarding the situation.

Decree God's Word and watch Him move on your behalf. God honors His Word above all His name.

"Let no corrupt communication proceed out of your mouth, but that which is good to the use of edifying, that it may minister grace unto the hearers."

Ephesians 4:29 KJV

Paul was admonishing us about using damaging language. As saints we have to make better use of our words. We must replace the negative with positive. Our words should educate and enrich those who hear them, even us. They should minister kindness and refine the hearers.

Surely, we can speak the truth to one another in love. Apostle Paul admonishes us to do that. We also have to speak the truth in love, including ourselves.

Mistakes are going to happen in life; that is how we learn and grow. Yes, we all have come close but have fallen short of the glory of God. However, it is not a license to stay where we fall.

Constantly reminding ourselves of past mistakes and failures only hinders progress. Once we repent, God is faithful and just to forgive us.

We must remember the times that we had success and how God caused greatness to be established in our lives. Not only that, we must remember what God says about us; we can do all things through Christ who strengthens us. ALL things, not just what we want or what people say we are capable of. It begins with our faith and trust in God. Trust God to enlighten you with new understanding.

We can begin by filling our vocabulary with the Word of God. The more we speak God's Word it will become more prevalent in our lives. The manifestation of God's will and promises will be evident. In Colossians, Paul challenges us to put on the new man.

He instructs us to learn more of Christ that way we can be reestablished, so we can become like Him.

"And have put on the new man, which is renewed in knowledge after the image of Him that created him."

Colossians 3:10 KJV

Let's put on a new way of thinking. The Word says let the mind that is in Christ be in us also.

The more that we get into the Word of God, the more our thoughts will reflect His thoughts. We can and must embrace the mind of Christ.

Knowing the Word of God gives us the proper vocabulary to speak effectively. God honors His Word above all His name.

The power of death and life is in the tongue. We can either destroy or create with the words that we speak. We need to be able to articulate the Word of God. We will be able to get all He has in store for us once we learn to do this. The strength of faith in God will fulfill our request. Our faith is the assurance that we will receive that which we ask God for in prayer.

The prayer of a righteous person is powerful and effective.

James 5:16 NIV

I like how the Amplified Bible puts this verse from James. It says "The heartfelt and persistent prayer of a righteous man can accomplish much [when put into action and made effective by God—it is dynamic and can have tremendous power.]" Whatsoever we ask in faith believing, we shall receive. It's not enough to speak it; we have to believe that which we speak James 5:16 AMP.

Faith

We cannot doubt. We have to trust in the Lord wholeheartedly that He will move on the level of faith that we have. God has dealt to every man the measure of faith and even a minuscule amount is powerful.

"If ye have faith as a grain of a mustard seed, ye shall say unto this mountain, remove hence to yonder place; and it shall remove and nothing shall be impossible unto you."

Matthew 17:20 KJV

That is remarkable! We have been allotted that much power with faith and the words of our mouth. There is no reason that the people of God should surrender their right to speak greatness into their lives. Now is the time to exercise authority over our minds and the words of our mouths.

Let the mind that is in Christ also be in us. We have to start thinking of ourselves as God thinks of us.

He gave His only Son in order for us to live abundantly. It is time to walk into that abundance and start decreeing the promises of God over our lives. We will have the promises given us according to our faith.

When God gave EVERYONE faith to believe He also gave power to decide what to have faith in. I choose to put all my faith in God and His promises. Use your measure! If it's smaller than you want, exercise it, build it up. When we place our faith in God, we are working on it. We will see results as change and growth occur. Decide where you are putting your faith and make it stay there until the work produces the desired results.

"Verily, verily I say unto, He that believeth on me, the works that I do shall he do also; and greater works than these shall he do; because I go unto my Father."

John 14:12 KJV

Jesus was speaking of his disciples and telling them that they were capable of performing the great works as He had done. We being followers of Christ are capable of the same. The mountains have to move when we say so; Peace has to come in turbulent situations when we speak. Health has to be restored when we declare the Word. This is accomplished according

to the power that works within us; which is through Christ
Jesus.

David is a prime example of how to apply this concept. King
Saul had some discouraging words to David about fighting
Goliath. David did not allow King Saul's words to dictate
his future.

"David said to Saul Let no man's heart fail on account of
him; your servant will go and fight the Philistine. Then
Saul said to David, you are not able to go against this
Philistine to fight with him; for you are but a youth, and
he a man of war from his youth."

1 Samuel 17:32-33 KJV

David did not allow the words that were spoken about him
determine the outcome of his life and decisions. Saul judged
the situation by what he could see. We have to have faith to
believe what God can do. God is the creator of all heaven
and earth. God is omnipotent, omniscient, omnipresent, and
Almighty. We cannot limit God by how we feel or what we
see. David stopped to consider the possibilities of God instead
of how impossible the circumstance appeared.

"David said moreover, The Lord that delivered me out of the paw of the lion, and out of the paw of the bear, he will deliver me out of the hand of this Philistine."

1 Samuel 17:37 KJV

David spoke with boldness and trusted in the Lord. He realized the obvious, but he did not accept that as the final result. God's Word says we are to speak those things that be not as though they are. David's words coupled with his faith allowed him to create an atmosphere for God to move. We should emulate David in this aspect.

Before we speak, we have to remember that we are held accountable for every word. Once we come to the realization that we can establish events, then we can properly use what God has given us.

We have the power and authority to speak and decree into the atmosphere. Now is the time to grab a hold of this revelation and start speaking to the giants and giant-sized situations in our lives. The God that brought us out of every other major situation is the same God that can get us out of every situation that we may face presently or in the future.

Jesus also applied the strategy of decreeing a thing and seeing it established. He literally caused a shift in the atmosphere.

Speaking to the storm showed how Jesus used the power of words to alter a situation. Regardless of the reaction that others around Him, Jesus knew how to handle the situation. He used his words to reconstruct the atmosphere.

"And when he was entered into a ship, his disciples followed him, And behold, arose a great tempest in the sea, insomuch that the ship was covered with the waves: but he was asleep. And his disciples came to him, and awoke him, saying Lord, save us: we perish. And he saith unto them, why are ye fearful, O ye of little faith? Then he rose, and rebuked the winds and the sea and there was a great calm. But the men marveled, saying, what manner of man is this, that even the winds and the sea obey him?"

Matthew 8:23-27 KJV

"And there arose a great storm of wind, and the waves beat into the ship, so that it was now full. And he was in the hinder part of the ship, asleep on a pillow: and they awake him, and say unto him, Master, carest thou not that we perish? And he arose, and rebuked the wind, and said unto the sea, Peace be still. And the wind ceased, and there was a great calm."

Mark 4:37-39 KJV

Both scriptures reference the same occasion. A great storm came and caught the men on board off guard.

Jesus was not rattled by the situation, instead he took control. He spoke directly to the storm, rebuked it and told it to cease. He did not cower at the tumultuous winds.

He stood firm on the power and authority he was given and adjusted the atmosphere with his words.

We are children of God; we have the power to do miraculous things with our speech just as Jesus did, if we believe in him.

"Verily, verily, I say unto you, He that believeth on me, the works that I do shall he do also; and greater works than these shall he do; because I go unto my Father."

John 14: 12 KJV

Only the sons and daughters of God have access to this power. It is of necessity that we have complete faith and trust in the Father.

We cannot speak one thing from our mouths and doubt our words in our minds. The Word of the Lord says ask in faith, believing, then you will receive.

Faith the size of a mustard seed can move mountains, but the faith must be evident. Faith is the substance of things hoped for, the evidence of things not seen. Our hope must be in God and he will manifest the outcome.

"And Jesus answering saith unto them, Have faith in God. For verily I say unto you, that whosoever shall say unto this mountain, Be thou removed, and be thou cast into the sea; and shall not doubt in his heart, but shall believe that those things which he saith shall come to pass; he shall have whatsoever he saith."

Mark 9: 23 KJV

God's word informs us of this several times. The key is how to properly exercise these rights. Jesus explained it here to his disciples. We have to use our faith. Our words coupled with our faith brings results. Our trust and faith in God is what accomplishes the changing of situations. The Greater One, our Heavenly Father lives in us and His Spirit is where the power comes from. When we realize that the Spirit of God working in us empowers our speech, we can exercise our right to decree and see things become established.

We have to believe and speak without any doubt. Our words have to boldly resound into the atmosphere, forcibly creating change. That mountain that stands between us and God's plans for our lives has to move. Whether it be test, obstacle, distraction, person, place, or thing; it has to move.

Who better to put it in its proper place than the ones who have to face it? Yes, us! You and I. Declare God's Word and promises over your mountain and watch it be removed.

Some circumstances may seem as colossal as a mountain. Stop! Before you speak on the situation, consider a few things. Nothing is impossible for the God we serve! He is the Creator of all Heaven and Earth. The Bible says, the Earth is the Lord's and the fullness thereof and they that dwell therein. With the Earth as His footstool, how difficult are the decisions we face. God is the author and finisher of our faith; surely, He knows how to handle a mountain. His Word says to acknowledge Him in all our ways and He will direct our path. The Word of God is our direction, our script for speaking to life's trials.

"Let the words of my mouth, and the meditation of my heart, be acceptable in thy sight, O Lord, my strength, and my redeemer."

Psalm 19: 14 KJV

David was petitioning God to guide his word and thoughts. He was determined to live a life that was pleasing to God. David realized that God was able to give him the right way to think and speak. Knowing that God holds us responsible for every word that we say, it's only wise to seek His counsel before we speak.

We should do the same for the deep thoughts that come from within our hearts. As we seek guidance from God, He will lead us down the path of righteousness. The Word of God tells us that wisdom is the principal thing (Proverbs 4:7). We have to use wisdom when we speak.

It makes no sense to say something and then later think you should not have said it.

If we think first and then speak, we eliminate the process of retracing our words, ensuring we responded the best way possible.

"The tongue of the righteous speaketh wisdom ..."

Psalm 37:30 KJV

In this text David was contrasting the wicked and the righteous. If we are going to be right in God's eyes, we have to look to Him for wisdom.

Righteousness is simply the quality of being morally right and acting in a moral way. In our pursuit of righteousness, we should speak wisdom. What is wisdom?

Wisdom- the quality of being wise; good judgment; the state of being informed and learned; prudent

Our speech has to reflect good judgment. The language we use must show that we are well informed and learned. The Word of God says that wisdom is the principal thing; therefore, get wisdom: and with all thy getting get understanding.

Remember we are held accountable for every idle word, which means our speech should have credibility. We must stop and think before we speak.

Heart and Mind

"For as he thinketh in his heart, so is he..."

Proverbs 23:7 KJV

The heart and mind work together to bring forth our thoughts. These are cogitations; deep thoughts that come from within us. Our words are a reflection of these collaborative efforts. Both our heart and mind possess great power. We have the ability to reconfigure these areas so that they produce new results. Let us deal with the heart and mind.

The heart is an intricate and sensitive part of us. It is said to be our core. The heart is the center of emotions, our innermost thoughts, and feelings. Emotions are strong reactions or agitation of feelings such as love, hate, fear, and anger.

"Keep thy heart with all diligence; for out of it are the issues of life"

Proverbs 4:23 KJV

I love Proverbs 4:23 CEV. It says "carefully guard your thoughts because they are the source of true life." We must realize our emotions are a gauge, not the guideline for our lives.

Matthew 12:34-35 MSG says "it's your heart, not the dictionary that gives meaning to your words. A good person produces good deeds and words season after season. An evil person is blight on an orchard." Matthew 12:34-35 GNT puts it like this: "The mouth speaks what the heart is full of." Matthew 12:36 AMP informs us that "on the day of judgment people will have to give and accounting for every careless and useless word they speak." I love to read different versions to get a greater perspective. We clearly have to have our hearts healthy in order to speak life and good into our lives.

We cannot change our words and expect our hearts to follow suit. We must deal with the root of the issues by taking inventory of what is in our hearts. Both things from our past and present can affect what type of words we are speaking. The evidence from our concerns in life will manifest.

It is imperative that we address those issues before we can make a change in our speech. We will know what and how to make adjustments once we find the root of our feelings concerning life.

Opinions, awareness, or sentiment are words used to describe feelings. These functions of the heart combine and take part in forming thoughts which take place in the mind.

Our mind is just as complex as our heart, if not more. The mind is the seat of consciousness, in which thinking occurs. It is intellect, reason, and psyche. This is where the governing of our actions takes place. Our mind and heart guide our lives. The health and state of those parts of us will shape how we perceive ourselves and others.

The way that we think of ourselves will make us. And though we are not to think more highly of ourselves than we ought, we have to see ourselves as God sees us.

He loves us so much that he sent His only Son to die for us. We are pretty special in God's sight. The moment we accepted Him into our hearts as Lord we were made part of His family. That means we are royalty. We are joint heirs with Christ. Do our thoughts match our position?

"But you are a chosen generation, a royal priesthood, a holy nation, a peculiar people; that ye should show forth the praises of him who has called you out of darkness into his marvelous light: Which in time past were not obtained mercy, but now have obtained mercy."

1 Peter 2:9 KJV

We must realize as Christians, "we are the ones chosen by God, chosen for the high calling of priestly work, chosen to be a holy people, God's instruments to do His work and speak out for Him to tell others the night -and- day difference He made for us- from nothing to something, from rejected to accepted." That is from 1 Peter 2:9 MSG.

Our speech must reflect who we are and where we are. We are a royal priesthood and a holy nation. We are seated in heavenly places in Christ Jesus. When we allow God to be seated on the throne of our hearts, He will give us a better way of thinking. We cannot make the change on our own. Proverbs 16:3 AMP says "commit your works to the Lord [submit and trust them to Him], And your plans will succeed [if you respond to His will and guidance].

God can bring about a new and improved method for thinking. When we allow God to order our thoughts we will get a renewed perspective of the situations that we face. His Word says we are to acknowledge Him in all our ways and He will direct our path.

God knows your thoughts anyway, why not make Him Lord of your thoughts. He should already be Lord over our lives. Making Jesus lord over our heart and over our mind will just yield us keys for productive speech.

Learning how to reply during conversation and responding to circumstances may not be easy, but with God all things are possible. God will instruct us in our speech. When we seek His face, we can ask for directions.

In Psalms 19:14 AMP, David requested God to let the words of his mouth and the meditations of his heart to be acceptable to God. Study His Word; there are other times that God gave the words that were to be spoken.

Proverbs 15:28 AMP says" the heart of the righteous thinks carefully about how to answer [in a wise and appropriate and timely way], But the [babbling] mouth of the wicked pours out malevolent things.

This text is saying do not just answer without considering the entirety of the question or all the factors. We must use effective communication. We have to take into account who we are speaking to and what is actually being asked, as well as the effects of how we answer.

If a parent asks a child where have you been?; "out" is not the best answer to give. The correct way to handle the situation is to stop and think about a respectful way to answer including the details that are required.

As a parent I want to know where you were, who you were with, and what you did when you were there?

Once you have come up with a response, then consider the consequences of that reaction. These simple steps give us better choices in our statements. That does not mean everyone is always going to agree with the way we choose to speak and respond.

As we make every effort to speak the truth in love to each other and to ourselves, we know we did as the Lord asked.

Even if it is not a parent and child situation, the same rules apply. It may be a boss/employee, teacher/student, or leader/ministry, but we must consider the answer before we release the response.

According to Proverbs 16:23 MSG They make a lot of sense, these wise folks;whenever they speak, their reputation increases. Let's choose to be wise in our speech.

God downloaded so many golden nuggets into Solomon about speech. The heart of our father is for us to be like Him. His words create, teach, and edify. Our words should possess those same characteristics. Once we study and seek His face, God will reveal His heart. We then should ask for Him to make our heart like His. After we acquire the heart of the Father our thoughts will align with His as well. We just have to allow God to change us into who He would have for us to be. God used so many for His purpose, surely, He can use us. God has no respect of persons. Trust and faith in him is key.

Eating Words

"Either make the tree good, and his fruit good; or else make the tree corrupt, and his fruit corrupt: for the tree is known by his fruit."

Matthew 12:33 KJV

A man's belly is satisfied with the fruit of his mouth; and with the increase of his lips shall he be filled. Death and life are in the power of the tongue: those who love it shall eat the fruit thereof.

Proverbs 18:20-21 KJV

The saying that "you are what you eat" says it in simplest form. In the natural, when we eat it affects our physical state. What we eat affects us sometimes for the good and sometimes for the bad. Our diet builds our health and body, however at other times it can cause problems. The same is true for our verbal meal. We are affected spiritually with our language appetite. Solomon made it clear that we will have to deal with the consequences of our words.

God has given us the power to either speak life or death. We are going to experience what we produce with our mouths. The more we speak edifying, Godly language the more we are satisfied with the results they produce. After continuing to speak a certain way over time we become convinced in what we are saying.

The issues and feelings that are planted in our hearts grow. When our language is based on those seeds, we start bearing corresponding fruit. Our fruit should be ripe, but could it be rotten? Does it bear life or does it bring death? Whichever it is, our bellies will be satisfied with it.

Life and death are in our words. When we choose to speak positively with words of affirmation, we can decree life. God's Word brings life.

When we declare the Word of the Lord on a regular basis, we will see life manifested into our circumstances. Remember God sent His only Son to die that we may have life and life more abundantly. The Word of God will go forth to produce life on our behalf.

We must remember that our words also can cause death. Negativity and doubt, in a situation where positivity and faith are required to achieve desired results, brings fatality.

We do not ever want to be the cause of something good being cancelled. Our thoughts and words if not carefully chosen can do that.

The bible references how Jesus limited what He did in Nazareth because of the unbelief of the people. The people were responding out of familiarity.

They thought they knew who He was. It is similar to how we assume we are familiar with how things are going to turn out or how we should respond. We limit God when we do not allow Him to be God. He is the author and finisher of our faith. He knows what is going on with us, but we have free will.

Either we can trust Him to work all things together for our good, or we can try to work things together on our own. If we think we have it, He will allow us to see that we really do not. Our thoughts and words will reflect on whether we trust Him to work on our behalf. We cannot allow unbelief to push God out of our speech.

We have to speak God's Word over our lives. God says to meditate on His Word day and night. As we do this His words become what we speak on a regular basis.

What we deposit will be available for us to withdraw as we need it. The Word of God is our daily bread. Eat the word, take it in, and savor it. Give God permission to fulfill your appetite with His Word.

As we ingest the Word we are being filled with power. The power to decree life where it is needed and death to where it is needed. Eat the daily bread and watch God honor His Word.

Our words hold so much power. Power can be very dangerous if it is not used in an appropriate way. The scripture and various parables have given us proof of what verbal declarations can achieve. Once we apply the wisdom, knowledge, and understanding of God's word to our speech we will be able to use our speech to recreate our world.

The key to the power lies in God, the author and finisher of our faith. He wrote the script and He releases the power that causes our words to be established. We have the power to decree a thing and it shall be established, created, enacted, or built.

"Commit thy way unto the Lord; trust also in him; and he shall bring it to pass."

Psalm 37:5 KJV

Moses had to commit and trust in God. Moses was not secure in his speaking capabilities and he let God know. God reminded Moses that it was He who made man's mouth.

In Exodus 4:12 KJV, God informs Moses that He will teach him what to say. God has a plan for us as well. The question is will we seek Him for directions?

Make the decision to trust in the Lord and the power of His might. Have faith in His Word and know that it will accomplish that which it is set out to do. God has given us power to create with our words. Let us take time to study His Word and build our faith, before we speak.

Secret Weapons

"THE WORD WAS GOD!"

What I am about to share has been hidden in plain sight. I have heard these words most of my life. One day after hearing someone read it aloud, the light bulb came on.

"In the beginning was the Word, and the Word was with God, and the Word was God."

John 1:1 KJV

Let me explain. God does not change! So, what does that mean? God still is His word. When we speak God's word, we make a decision to bring Him into whatever situation we are dealing with at the time. He is The Creator. He knows the best way to handle our lives. God even assures us that His word; He himself will make sure it is done.

I got a better understanding of God becoming present through speaking His existence into my family. There is nothing like being able to see results when you go to God in prayer. His word says when we ask in prayer through faith believing, you will receive. God honors his word above all His name.

There are so many times I can recall, but none as impactful as when my husband became ill. Jeffrey had been working consistently at church and home. Over the course of a few months he kept seeming to be dehydrated and having to go to the emergency room. At that time I would pray God heal him and take away the pain. That doesn't seem bad does it? I didn't think so. After that type of prayer, he ended up back in the ER two more times.

Well, the last time I remember him going to the ER he asked me to pray as he always does, but this time was different. I was completely fed up with going to the ER and I was frustrated with praying passively. I intensified.

This time when I spoke to God in prayer it was filled with his word.

I told God what His word said! "God, you said healing is the children's bread!" "You said by YOUR stripes we are healed." "YOU said that we can decree a thing and it shall be established." YOU said you would not withhold any good thing from us."

"YOU said, many are the afflictions of the righteous but, YOU would deliver us out of them all." YOU said if we ask in faith believing, we shall receive." "Father, YOU said whatever we ask in JESUS name shall be done!" "God, You said your word will not go out and return to you void, but it will accomplish what you have sent it to do!"

My husband has not had to go back to the hospital for that same issue since then. The difference between my first prayers and my last prayer was God. I gave Him His word. I put God in the situation and He dealt with sickness. It is imperative that we remember that God honors His word above His name. Jesus is the name higher than any other name. Philippians 2:10 tells us that the things in the earth must bow at the name of Jesus. If it can be named, it must bow when Jesus name is spoken.

Bowing is a way to show respect. God is all powerful which means there has to be respect when His name is spoken. The Bible tells us that whoever calls on the name of the Lord shall be saved. When we say "Jesus!" we are calling Him. When we speak His word, we are calling on Him. Remember, the Word was God; that is one of His names. He honors Himself above His name by doing exactly what is written about Him.

In Isaiah 55:11 CEV, it says that's how it is with my words. They don't return to me without doing everything I send them to do.

We have to remember that God is not like man, He cannot lie. He does not have to repent like us. Everything He says happens and the promises He makes, He keeps.

God is faithful, unfailing, and true. I could go on and on because that is how I know Him. God has never failed me!

Once I realized that speaking, praying, and meditating on His word was adding Him into the equation of my life I was elated!

I don't know about you, but I cannot fix my life by rambling off the top of my head. I need help to get my mind and heart together before I say something. Otherwise, I have to either apologize to someone or apologize to myself for speaking out of emotion.

When I speak God's word, He goes to accomplish His will for me. I know that God has great thoughts and plans for us to prosper. God shows His power when we use His word and His word prevails; He prevails.

In a nutshell, God's word is Himself. Speaking God's word is inserting Him into what we are talking about. The goal is not to say words that we think sound good or to manipulate words to get a result that we want.

Our words do create and change our lives, but not always with the best outcome. We will get the most effective results from what we speak when we use God as The Word whom He is.

The biggest secret weapon is God! We can achieve a positive change by carefully choosing our words. The most impactful change will occur when God is the source of our words. We make God the source of our words when we realize that He is the source of our lives. Understanding the source helps us to determine purpose. After the purpose is grasped, then we can better make use of what we have.

The second secret weapon is knowledge. We have all heard the saying "knowledge is power" and" when you know better do better." I had to stop and consider those points. What other knowledge have I gained about on this subject? What else can I learn about the effects of words on people? Are there any natural or physical effects of speech?

All these questions began to flood my mind. God reminded me that I had learned about this during some training sessions for work. The training itself was not the point, I needed to gain answers. It was a single golden nugget during a session on working with children who face trauma that sparked a hunger for further information.

Our instructor Patrice informed us that what we say and how we say it can trigger something in the brain. I immediately had questions. What type of trigger? What happens when it is triggered? How are we affected by this trigger? Can we counteract this reaction? I had to know.

My burning desire to find answers lead me to a few more training sessions and ultimately to a book called *Words Can Change Your Brain* by Andrew Newberg and Mark Robert Waldman. I actually reached out to Dr. Waldman in regards to understanding the power of words and his research. The information I found was amazing.

In *Words Can Change Your Brain,* it was explained that there can be an immediate interruption of neuro functioning of our brains. Neuro changes in the brain occur that influence logic, reason, language processing by what we say and how we say it.

Dr. Waldman and Newberg really explained how large of an impact negative words can have on our health, mentally and physically. The good thing is positive words can have a great deal of influence as well. Dr. Waldman shared with me that there is research being done that also supports this information. The more positive we speak the greater the impact.

Nothing is more positive than decreeing the word of the Lord. The bible is filled with the will and promises of the Lord concerning his people. It is his will that none perish but all come to repentance. He did not send his son to condemn us but to save the world. No weapon formed against us shall prosper for that is the inheritance of his servants. He will never leave nor forsake us. All things work together for the good of those that love God and are called according to his purpose. He daily loads us with benefits. In his presence is the fullness of joy and at his right hand treasures forever more. Goodness and mercy shall follow us all the days of our lives. He will not have us lack any good thing. It is his will that we prosper and be in good health even as our souls prosper. He sends the Holy Spirit to be our comforter. Don't get me started on the many names he possesses that he honors.

In all our gaining of wisdom and knowledge, we must also get an understanding. In doing so, remember to trust in the Lord with all your heart and lean not to your own understanding. Acknowledge him in all your ways and he will direct you. We gain the greatest revelation in our time with God. Time in prayer, service, and study all allow for the opportunity to encounter God for the release of his wisdom. Wisdom comes from the lips of those with understanding. Lord, make the words of our mouth and the meditations of our hearts be acceptable in your sight. Remind us the be quick to listen and slow to speak, that we make better use of our word power.

Understanding the power of our words will change our lives forever. We must go through the process and take our time to consider and understand the effects of our words before we speak.

Reconstruction

"And be not conformed to this world: but be ye transformed by the renewing of your mind, that ye may prove what is that good, and acceptable, and perfect will of God.

Romans 12:2 KJV

Reconstruction can begin when we are determined to take the necessary actions for a thorough change. Complete attention to every detail is imperative in this process. Our will, heart, and mind all have to be yielded to the Spirit of God.

The above verse makes clear to us that we can not become adapted to the culture we are immersed in; but instead, decide to make the modifications for our minds to be made anew. We must start by asking God to create in us a clean heart and renew his right spirit within us.

What this does is invite God to upgrade us to a righteous, moral, and honorable character. Not to say we didn't have it before; now it is just being elevated to a new level as we shift.

As our heart and mind undergo this transformation we will begin to see evidence in our speech. Our entire lives will be set on a new course. The tongue is but a small part of the body, yet it has such a huge impact on our life.

"A small rudder on a huge ship in the hands of a skilled captain sets the course in the face of the strongest winds. A word out of your mouth may seem of no account, but it can accomplish nearly anything-or destroy it! It only takes a spark, remember, to set off a forest fire. A careless or wrongly placed word out of your mouth can do that. By our speech we can ruin the world, turn harmony to chaos, throw mud on a reputation, send the whole world up in smoke and go up in smoke with it smoke right from the pit of hell."

James 3:4-6 MSG

Bullseye! Now that there is complete clarity, we have to adjust for the future. The word of God is what we have to speak, meditate on, and engrave on our hearts. The renewal comes when we allow the washing of the water of the word to remove what we don't need and supply all that is a necessity to have effective change in our speech.

The sole purpose of this book is to make known and understood that our words are powerful. God is the only way for us to learn to use our words in a way that will shape our future into what He originally purposed for our lives.

Remember, He is His word and when we take it to heart and employ it we will see results. God can't lie and He promised to do exceeding abundantly above all we can ask or think.

Take the initiative to try God and see if He won't open the windows of heaven and pour out blessings that there won't even be enough room to possess. I encourage you to follow through with putting into action what applicable.

Use the scriptures found throughout the book and take time to study a few that are specific to your particular season. Allow time for change to take place. James 1:4 ASV says "and let patience have *its* perfect work, that ye may be perfect and entire, lacking in nothing." Patience will surely be needed, but let it completely develop so that there will be no insufficiencies. Remember to always stop and think, "Before You Speak."

"For ye have need of patience, that, after ye have done the will of God, ye might receive the promise."

Hebrews 10:36 KJV

The following scriptures are for clarity, affirmations that will strengthen you during this transition. The word of God is full of many more. These will get you started, but I encourage you to continue to search for what you need for specific situations. There are apps, online resources, and books that are designed to have scriptures pertaining to exact topics of interest. As you progress, begin to search the Word for greater wisdom, knowledge, and understanding.

"Thou shall decree a thing, and it shall be established unto thee, and the light shall shine upon thy ways."
Job 22:28 KJV

I am purposed that my mouth shall not transgress.
Psalm 17:3 KJV

Let the words of my mouth, and the meditation of my heart, be acceptable in thy sight, O Lord, my strength, and my redeemer.
Psalm 19:14 KJV

For he spake, and it was done; he commanded, and it stood fast
Psalm 33:9 KJV

Commit thy way unto the Lord; trust also in him; and he shall bring it to pass.
Psalm 37:5 KJV

I will take heed to my ways, that I sin not with my tongue, I will keep my mouth with a bridle...
Psalm 39:1 KJV

The tongue of the righteous speaks wisdom ...
Psalm 37:30 KJV

My mouth shall speak wisdom; and the meditation of my heart shall be of understanding.
Psalm 49:3 KJV

Your word is a lamp unto my feet, and a light unto my path
Psalm 119:105 KJV

Make me to understand the way of your precepts: so shall I talk of your wondrous works.
Psalm 119:27 KJV

The entrance of thy words give light: it gives understanding unto the simple.
Psalm 119:30 KJV

Give me understanding, and I shall keep your law, yes, I shall observe it with my whole heart.
Psalm 119:34 KJV

Thou are my portion, O Lord: I have said that I would keep thy words.
Psalm 119:57 KJV

Thy word is true from the very beginning and every one of thy righteous judgments endureth for ever
Psalm 119:60 KJV

My tongue shall speak thy word: for all thy commandments are righteousness.
Psalm 119:72 KJV

For ever, O Lord thy word is settled in heaven.
Psalm 119:89 KJV

Through thy precepts I get understanding
Psalm 119:104 KJV

Set a watch, O Lord, before my mouth; keep the door of my lips
Psalm 141:3 KJV

Wisdom is the principal thing; therefore get wisdom: and with all thy getting get understanding.
Proverbs 4:7 KJV

Get wisdom, get understanding: forget it not; neither decline from the words of my mouth
Proverbs 4:5 KJV

Keep thy heart with all diligence; for out of it are the issues of life.
Proverbs 4:23 KJV

In the lips of him that has understanding wisdom is found
Proverbs 10:13 KJV

The heart of the righteous studieth to answer ...
Proverbs 15:28 KJV

The heart of the wise teacheth his mouth, addeth learning to
his lips
Proverbs 16:23 KJV

He that hath knowledge spare his words...
Proverbs 17:27 KJV

Whoso keepeth his mouth keepeth and tongue, keepeth his
soul from troubles.
Proverbs 21:23 KJV

For as he thinks in his heart, so is he...
Proverbs 23:7 KJV

Apply thine heart to instruction, and thine ears to words of
knowledge.
Proverbs 23:12 KJV

The Lord God hath given me the tongue of the learned, that
I should know how to speak a word in season to him that is

weary: he waken morning by morning; he waken my ear to hear as the learned.
Isaiah 50:4 KJV

No weapon that is formed against thee shall prosper; and every tongue that shall rise against thee in judgment thou shalt condemn. This is the heritage of the servants of the Lord, and their righteousness is of me, saith the Lord.
Isaiah 54:17 KJV

But seek ye first the kingdom of God, and his righteousness; and all these things shall be added unto you.
Matthew 6:33 KJV

For out of the abundance of the heart the mouth speaks.
Matthew 12:34b KJV

If ye have faith as a grain of a mustard seed, ye shall say unto this mountain, Remove hence to yonder place; and it shall remove and nothing shall be impossible unto you.
Matthew 17:20 KJV

And Jesus answering saith unto them, *Have faith in God. For verily I say unto you, That whosoever shall say unto this mountain, Be thou removed, and be thou cast into the sea; and shall not doubt in his heart, but shall believe that those things which he saith shall come to pass; he shall have whatsoever he saith.*
Mark 11: 23 KJV

For a good tree brings not forth corrupt fruit; neither does corrupt tree brings forth good fruit. For every tree is known by his own fruit. For the thorns men do not gather figs, nor of a bramble bush gather they grapes. A good man out of the good treasure of his heart brings forth that which is good; and an evil man out of the evil treasure of his heart brings forth that which is evil: for of the abundance of the heart the mouth speaks.
Luke 6:43-45 KJV

And calleth those things which be not as though they were
Romans 4: 17 KJV

And be not conformed to the ways of this world: but be ye transformed by the renewing of your mind, that ye may prove what is that good, and acceptable, and perfect, the will of God.
Romans 12:2 KJV

Casting down imaginations, and every high thing that exalts itself against the knowledge of God and bringing into captivity every thought to the obedience of Christ;
2 Corinthians 10:5 KJV

(By grace we are saved;) And has raised us up together and made us sit together in heavenly places in Christ Jesus
Ephesians 2:5b-6 KJV

And be renewed in the spirit of your mind
Ephesians 4:23 KJV

Let no corrupt communication proceed out of your mouth, but that which is good to the use of edifying, that it may minister grace unto the hearers.
Ephesians 4:29 KJV

Finally, be strong in the Lord and in the power of his might.
Ephesians 6:10 KJV

Let this mind be in you, which was also in Christ Jesus
Philippians 2:5 KJV

Finally, brethren, whatsoever things are true, whatsoever things are honest, whatsoever things are just, whatsoever things are pure, whatsoever things are lovely, whatsoever things are of good report; if there be any virtue, and if there be any praise, think on these things.
Philippians 4:8 KJV

I can do all things through Christ which strengthens me.
Philippians 4:13 KJV

And having put on the new man, which is renewed in knowledge after the image of him that created him.
Colossians 3: 10 KJV

Pray without ceasing.
1 Thessalonians 5:17 KJV

Wherefore, my beloved brethren, let every man be swift to hear, slow to speak, slow to wrath
James 1:19 KJV

Behold also the ships, which though they be so great, are driven of fierce winds, yet are they turned about with a very small helm, whithersoever the governor list.
James 3:4-5 KJV

Out of the same mouth proceed blessings and cursings. My brethren this should not be.
James 3:10 KJV

But you are a chosen generation, a royal priesthood, a holy nation, a peculiar people; that you should show forth the praises of him who has called you out of the darkness into his marvelous light.
1 Peter 2:9 KJV

Notes

When this book began the point was to help people understand how much power they possess within to change their world with words. Dr. Waldman and I agree that words create a specific attitude in parts of your brain but many other steps must be taken to change a life. I would be remiss if I didn't offer you the greatest power there is; salvation through Jesus Christ. This is a major decision, yet so simple and rewarding. God gave us Jesus as the key to unlocking how to effectively use His power to have our best life.

Salvation starts with your words. Simply ask for forgiveness of sins and the wrong things in your life. There is no condemnation to those who are in Christ Jesus. He's not there to point out the wrong. He allows his blood to cover the sins, blot it out. Verbally, confess that you believe that Jesus died on the cross for the sins and God raised Jesus from the dead.

if you confess with your mouth Jesus is Lord, and believe in your heart that God has raised Him from the dead, you will be saved.

Romans 10:9 NIV

The changes come in word and in deed, but by your decision. The next phase is repentance, which means to have remorse yes, but to turn from the old way of doing things. It is complete, wholehearted, unrestricted surrender to the Sovereign God. When we surrender to God we submit to his authority in actions, thoughts, and speech.

For God so loved the world, that he gave his only begotten son that whosoever believeth in him shall not perish, but have everlasting life. For he sent not his Son into the world to condemn the world; but through him might be saved.

John 3:16-17 KJV

Invite Jesus into your life by asking Him to come and live in your heart as Lord. Once Jesus is Lord in your life you have the Instructor and Wonderful Counselor will guide you. The bible has the instruction necessary to maneuver this new access to power.

Once you have given your life to Christ, find a church home where you can grow and continue to build your relationship with God. Accepting Jesus into your life will give you access to guidance and direction. God honors His word above all His name. I pray you try God at His word and see the results that align with His will for your life. He is the Author and Finisher of our Faith. He will never leave you nor forsake you. Remember God is available to help you in this transition when you look to Him before you speak.

Printed in the United States
By Bookmasters